Score

You'll Be Back
from the Broadway musical *Hamilton*
By Lin-Manuel Miranda

Arrangement for Two Pianos / Eight Hands
by Melody Bober

*Dedicated to
Deborah Turnbull and her piano students,
who LOVE to play quartets.*

Words and Music by
Lin-Manuel Miranda
Arranged by Melody Bober

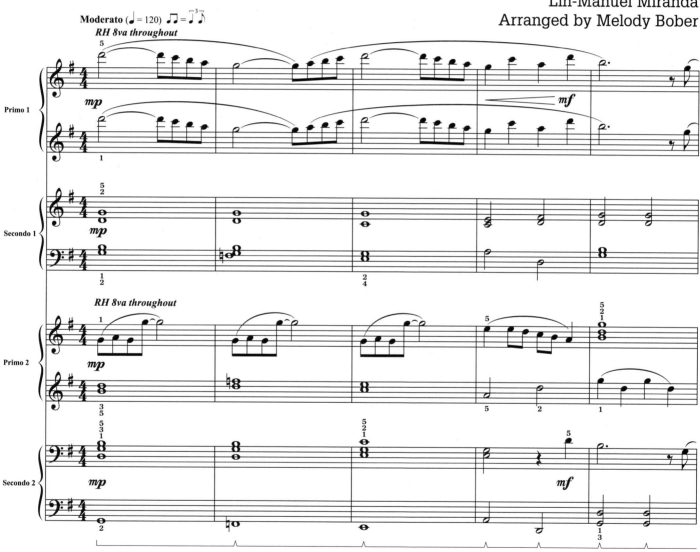

Produced by
Alfred Music
P.O. Box 10003
Van Nuys, CA 91410-0003
alfred.com

Printed in USA.

ISBN-10: 1-4706-4335-9
ISBN-13: 978-1-4706-4335-5